SCHIRMER'S LIBRARY
OF MUSICAL CLASSICS

Vol. 1980

T0033926

J.S. BACH

The "Goldberg" Variations

Piano or Harpsichord

(Kirkpatrick)

ISBN 978-0-7935-2245-3

G. SCHIRMER, *Inc.*

DISTRIBUTED BY
HAL•LEONARD®
CORPORATION
7777 W. BLUEMOUND RD. P.O. BOX 13819 MILWAUKEE, WI 53213

FACSIMILE OF THE ARIA IN THE ORIGINAL EDITION

CONTENTS

Keyboard Practice

Ed. 1614

consisting
of an

ARIA

with thirty variations
for the harpsichord
with 2 Manuals
Prepared for the Enjoyment
of Music-Lovers by

Johann Sebastian Bach

Edited for the harpsichord or piano
by Ralph Kirkpatrick

PREFACE

I
ORIGIN

The "Goldberg" Variations were first published in 1742 by Balthasar Schmid in Nürnberg under the modest title: "Keyboard-practice, consisting of an Aria with different variations for the harpsichord with two manuals. Prepared for the enjoyment of music-lovers by Johann Sebastian Bach, Polish royal and Saxon electoral court-composer, director and choir-master in Leipzig." The Aria appears as a Sarabande in Anna Magdalena Bach's notebook of the year 1725.

About the composition of these variations, Forkel[1] tells the following story, which, for all its doubtful character, has permanently attached to them the name of Bach's pupil, Johann Gottlieb Goldberg.[2]

"For this model, upon which all sets of variations should be formed (although for comprehensible reasons not a single set has yet been thus made), we have to thank the instigation of the former Russian ambassador to the electoral court of Saxony, Count Kaiserling,[3] who often stopped in Leipzig and brought there with him the afore-mentioned Goldberg, in order to have him given musical instruction by Bach. The Count was often ill and had sleepless nights. At such times, Goldberg, who lived in his house, had to spend the night in an antechamber, so as to play for him during his insomnia. Once the Count mentioned in Bach's presence that he would like to have some clavier pieces for Goldberg, which should be of such a smooth and somewhat lively character that he might be a little cheered up by them in his sleepless nights. Bach thought himself best able to fulfill this wish by means of Variations, the writing of which he had until then considered an ungrateful task on account of the repeatedly similar harmonic foundation. But since at this time all his works were already models of art, such also these variations became under his hand. Yet he produced only a single work of this kind. Thereafter the Count always called them *his* variations. He never tired of them, and for a long time sleepless nights meant: 'Dear Goldberg, do play me one of my variations.' Bach was perhaps never so rewarded for one of his works as for this. The Count presented him with a golden goblet filled with 100 *louis-d'or*. Nevertheless, even had the gift been a thousand times larger, their artistic value would not yet have been paid for."

II
FORM

Like an enormous passacaglia, these variations reiterate the harmonic implications of the same bass in thirty different forms. This fundamental bass is never stated entirely in its most elemental form, as quoted here (Ex. 1), not even in the Aria. But on this harmonic skeleton and around it are constructed the variations, each highly organized and composed of independent thematic material. These follow one another in a symmetrical grouping like the beads of a rosary.

Certain alterations of the fundamental bass are to be found. For example, chords of the sixth are interchanged with their root positions, and *vice versa*. It even happens that a six-four is substituted for a sixth-

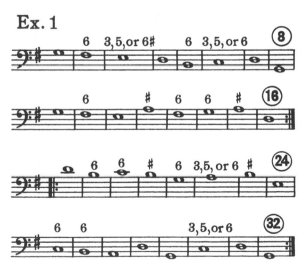

Ex. 1

[1] "Über Johann Sebastian Bachs Leben, Kunst und Kunstwerke", IX. (1802).
[2] See Ernst Dadder: "Johann Gottlieb Goldberg", *Bach-Jahrbuch*, 1923, p. 57.
[3] See Heinrich Miesner: "Graf v. Keyserlingk und Minister v. Happe, zwei Gönner der Familie Bach." *Bach-Jahrbuch*, 1934, p. 101.

chord. The bass, the third, the sixth, or even the fifth is occasionally sharped or flatted. In some places there is a certain interchange or ambiguous hesitation between the fifth and the sixth, with much use of the third alone against the bass, in order to leave this ambiguity free of limitation or definition. Frequently a basic chord is given a subordinate position but the main progression is reaffirmed by a kind of harmonic circumlocution; or a harmony, instead of being stated unequivocally once, is hinted at two or three times. This often occurs in passages where certain steps of the bass are displaced from the measures proper to them (especially in the canons) being either anticipated or retarded and bunched together at the close of a phrase. But all these devices are employed by Bach in such ways as never to obscure the main outlines. A detailed study of these variations to try to see exactly how Bach conceived their relation to a common foundation reveals more fully the intellectual span, the imagination, and the genius which permitted so much daring freedom.

The form of the Variations as a whole may be shown by comparison, as before, to that of a rosary, or perhaps better explained by an architectural analogy. Framed as if between two terminal pylons, one formed by the Aria and the first two variations, the other by the two penultimate variations and the Quodlibet, the Variations are grouped like the members of an elaborate colonnade. The groups are composed of a canon and an elaborate two-manual arabesque, enclosing in each case another variation of independent character. Following upon the pylon-like group which terminates this rhythmic procession, the Aria repeated closes the great circle.

There are nine canons, at intervals successively from the unison to the ninth, those at the fourth and fifth in contrary motion, that at the ninth without any independent third voice, such as accompanies the others. Among the variable forms are to be found a fughetta, a French overture, florid slow movements, etc.

The Quodlibet mixes together the tunes of two folk-songs:

> "Ich bin so lang nicht bei dir g'west.
>   Ruck her, ruck her, ruck her."

and:

> "Kraut und Rüben haben mich vertrieben.
>   Hätt, mein' Mutter Fleisch gekocht,
>   so wär ich länger blieben."

These might be translated thus:

> "I've not been with you for so long.
>   Come closer, closer, closer."

and:

> "Beets and spinach drove me far away.
>   Had my mother cooked some meat,
>   then I'd have stayed much longer."

Possibly this Quodlibet was associated in Bach's mind with the memory of those annual reunions of the Bach family described by Forkel[4]. "The way in which they passed the time during this meeting was entirely musical. Because the whole company was composed of cantors, organists, and town-musicians, who were all concerned with the Church, and because anyway it was still the custom to begin all things with religion, as soon as they were assembled a chorale was first struck up. From this devout beginning they proceeded to jokes which were frequently in strong contrast. That is, they then sang popular songs, partly of comic and also partly of indecent content, all mixed together on the spur of the moment so that the different improvised voices indeed constituted a kind of harmony, but so that the words in every voice were different. This kind of improvised harmonizing they called a Quodlibet, and not only could laugh over it quite whole-heartedly themselves, but also aroused just as hearty and irresistible laughter in all who heard them."

[4]*Op. cit.*

III
THE INSTRUMENT

The kind of instrument for which the Goldberg Variations were composed is perhaps best exemplified by the harpsichord believed (probably erroneously) to have belonged to Bach, now in the *Hochschule für Musik* in Berlin.[5] This instrument has two manuals and four sets of strings, likewise four sets of jacks (plucking mechanism), all furnished in quill. The lower manual controls two registers, one of a rather dark eight-foot tone (that is, at normal pitch) and one of sixteen-foot tone (that is, sounding an octave lower). The upper manual controls also two registers, one of a somewhat lighter eight-foot tone, and the other of four-foot tone (that is, sounding an octave higher). The registers of the upper manual may be connected to the lower by means of a coupler, operated by pushing in the upper manual. For the eight-foot strings of the upper manual there is a stop operating a set of pads which partially damp the tone, giving a lute-like effect. All the registers of this instrument are operated by hand stops. The tone is still quite full, of a rather clear, silvery character.

Some harpsichords had the four-foot stop on the lower manual, and the jacks of part or all the registers furnished in leather. Harpsichords with sixteen-foot tone seem to have been fairly rare. A very few harpsichords seem to have been constructed with pedals or *genouillères* (knee-levers) to facilitate quicker changing of registers.

Although some degree of accent may be obtained, and from sensitive instruments an appreciable difference in tone as well, according to the speed with which the string is plucked, really substantial nuances of tone volume are not obtainable through the touch of the fingers. But the very thinness of harpsichord tone makes possible the effectiveness of almost infinite degrees of *legato* and *staccato*, and by these means it is possible to give the illusion of increased dynamic variation, much as a painter can suggest the third dimension in a mere outline drawing.

The variety of registers makes possible the use of different tone colors for various sections, and the adding or subtracting of registers produces various degrees of volume. Also the two keyboards enable the player to employ two different qualities of tone at the same time. A kind of richness of which the piano is incapable is the full octave doubling produced throughout by the use of the four- and sixteen-foot stops. When these are used in conjunction with eight-foot tone, we have for every note struck the normal tone, the octave above, and the octave below sounding simultaneously.

The possibilities of harpsichord registration (so often misconstrued by pianists) are not to be employed in the service of pianistic chiaroscuro dynamics, but rather changes of register should be logically determined by musical construction so that they clarify rather than obscure musical form. Upon the resulting flat dynamic planes the utmost subtlety and expressiveness of phrasing must be employed. Between harpsichord and piano music one must acknowledge a difference of style analogous even if only at face value to the difference, let us say, between the painting of Botticelli and that of Titian.

Any thorough examination of the character of the harpsichord is enough, it would seem, to show that Bach, with however much approval he might have regarded the modern piano, would have composed for it altogether differently. By this time it should be universally realized that the keyboard music of Bach is not piano music, and that on the piano it must be regarded as transcription. If Bach is played on the piano, and if justice is to be done to the true expression of the thematic material and to an undistorted exposition of whole musical structure, a style of playing must be cultivated which will be quite different from the usual pianistic habits. Let us hope some elements of this style will become fairly clear in the course of the following discussions.

---

[5]See Georg Kinsky: "Zur Echtheitsfrage des Berliner Bach-Flügels", *Bach-Jahrbuch*, 1924, p. 128.

IV

ORNAMENTATION

Because of the almost incredible ignorance and false information prevalent concerning eighteenth-century ornamentation, it would have been desirable to undertake a comprehensive discussion of Bach's ornamentation, but the restrictions of space and subject limit us here to a statement of the most necessary generalities and leave to another occasion the quotation of many further important details from eighteenth-century treatises.

The understanding of a written explanation of harpsichord ornamentation, no matter how clear and accurate, has not been facilitated by the variety of signs used by different composers and their great inconsistency of nomenclature, or, needless to say, by the erroneous "traditions" inherited from the nineteenth century and maintained by aggressively ignorant musicians and writers. Moreover, only a thorough knowledge and experience of the harpsichord reveal all the many shades of variation of which ornaments are susceptible, and especially their manifold significance as accent, as means of continuity, as decoration incorporated in the melodic line, as enrichment of the musical fabric, or as expressive declamation. But through quotation from original tables and from eighteenth-century writers, and through additional comments and the written-out versions of ornaments in the Variations, the attempt has been made to convey to the reader as much as possible of the comparative clarity and sureness of mind which a careful study of the matter will permit.

In the "Clavier-Büchlein vor Wilhelm Friedemann Bach" Bach wrote out the table of ornaments which follows here.

Far more fruitful and adequate sources of information for Bach ornamentation are the books of Carl Philipp Emmanuel Bach ("Versuch über die wahre Art das Clavier zu spielen", First Part, 1753)[6] and of Johann Joachim Quantz ("Versuch einer Anweisung die Flöte traversière zu spielen", 1752).[6] From French works like the table of ornaments in d'Anglebert's harpsichord pieces (1689), St. Lambert's "Principes du Clavecin" (1702), and François Couperin's tables in his first book of harpsichord pieces (1713) and in "L'Art de toucher le clavecin" (1717)[7], we can also learn much that was taken over by German musicians, including Bach. A very useful source is the "Anleitung zum Clavierspielen" (1755) of Friedrich Wilhelm Marpurg. The "Klavierschule" of Daniel Gottlob Türk (1789, second edition 1802) is of less importance specifically for Bach, but forms a kind of summary of the whole of eighteenth-century German keyboard culture.

Standing out from the mass of modern falsification and confusion are two books concerned with musical ornamentation. "The Interpretation of the Music of the XVIIth and XVIIIth Centuries" by Arnold Dolmetsch (London, Novello) is quite indispensable and for the most part accurate, the work of one to whom anyone concerned with this music must be grateful. "Musical Ornamentation" by Edward Dannreuther (London, Novello) is somewhat more conveniently organized, but is unfortunately full of mistakes and inconsistencies in the section dealing with J. S. Bach. In fact it may be wise to warn the reader here against the frequent incorrectness and inaccuracy of Dannreuther's discussion and "corrections" of the ornaments in the Goldberg Variations, in spite of the general excellence of the book. Both works are composed mostly of quotations and paraphrases from the original treatises, and they nearly always permit distinction between primary sources and the sometimes doubtful conclusions of the compilers.

The abbreviated indication of ornaments has often been justified by the remark that it leaves clear the main harmonic and melodic progressions, and that the writing out of such an ornament as the mordent would in any case be an unnecessary complication of the text. But the principal reason for this incomplete expression of ornaments is a certain freedom of execution, not only in pieces where their choice and placing is left largely to the player, but even in works like the harpsichord pieces of François Couperin, where the composer indicates explicitly and consistently the precise ornaments which are to be performed by the player. This freedom comes on the one hand from the fresh impromptu character of much ornamentation, to which we have an illuminating contemporary parallel in American jazz, and on the other from the calculated subtle expressiveness of performance, which varies from instance to instance and from player to player, and makes it practically impossible to write out accurately the exact rhythmic form of certain trills, for example, or to generalize upon their execution beyond certain constant conditions. But these general conditions are very important and necessitate a training of the ear, and often a kind of declaration of independence from certain contrary modern practices. For the common eighteenth-century ornamentation, in spite of its freedom and subtlety, falls into certain definite categories and under certain general rules, a thorough knowledge of which is absolutely essential to anyone concerned with it. After enough experience one finds that seemingly arbitrary rules come to be thoroughly justified and explained by musical feeling.

We shall now proceed briefly to discuss these categories and rules in accordance with the clear codification and detailed accounts which are to be found in mid-century works like those of C. P. E. Bach, Marpurg, and Quantz.

GENERAL RULES

With certain rather rare and somewhat controversial exceptions, mostly of the earlier eighteenth-century (the passing appoggiatura or *Nachschlag*, for example, so much disliked by C. P. E. Bach), all ornaments are played on the beat; that is, they take their value from the beginning of the note affected by the sign, and the first note of the ornament will coincide with any note of the bass or any other voice which occurs on the same beat.

In canons or imitative passages the second voice should follow exactly the ornamentation of the first. (See C. P. E. Bach, Chap. II, Sect. 2, Par. 28.)

[6]Partial modern reprints. Leipzig, G. F. Kahnt.
[7]Modern reprint with English and German translations. Leipzig, Breitkopf & Härtel.

THE ORNAMENTS, INDIVIDUALLY TREATED

APPOGGIATURA (*Vorschlag, Accent, Port de voix*):
C. P. E. Bach distinguishes two kinds of appoggiatura,
one that is "long" and of variable length, and one
that is invariably "short".

According to general rule, a long appoggiatura
takes from the following note half or, in the case of
dotted notes, two thirds of its value (Ex. 2) but
rhythmic or harmonic considerations cause frequent
exceptions. (See the interesting and enlightening
examples in C. P. E. Bach and Quantz.) Moreover the
expression of certain appoggiaturas consists in their
improvisatory character and the fact that their value
is not exactly determinable.

Ex. 2 (R. L. K.)

The short appoggiatura, according to C. P. E.
Bach (Chap. II, Sect. 2, Par. 13), occurs most often
before short notes, but also before repeated notes and
before various figures where the melodic contour,
harmonic character, or rhythmic function is to be
preserved unchanged, such as at caesuras in connection with a quick note, and in syncopations, suspen-
sions, slurred passages, triplets, skips of thirds. He
gives many examples, more than can be quoted here.

C. P. E. Bach tries to indicate the duration of the
appoggiatura by the value of the small note, but most
composers, including his father, made little such
attempt.

PASSING APPOGGIATURA (*Nachschlag*): "The Passing
Appoggiaturas are found when several notes of the
same value descend by skips of thirds (Ex. 3a). They
must be played as seen at Ex. 3b." (Quantz, Chap.
VIII, Par. 6.)

Ex. 3 (Quantz, Tab. VI, Figs. 5, 6)

MORDENT (*Pincé*): Sometimes a distinction of notation is made between short and long mordents, ⟅
and ⟅, but it is scarcely ever followed consistently
(Ex. 4a.). The length of a mordent depends upon the
context and partly upon the value of the main note.
Sometimes the mordent prolongs itself through
several measures, becoming the *pincé continu* of
Couperin.

"There is another special way of making mordents
when they should be very short (Ex. 4b.). Of
these notes both struck simultaneously, one holds the
upper, immediately releasing the lower. This mode
is not to be neglected, as long as one employs it less
often than the other kinds of mordent. It occurs only
ex abrupto, that is, without connection." (C. P. E.
Bach, Chap. II, Sect. 5, Par. 3.)

Ex. 4 (Marpurg, Tab. V, Figs. 11a, 12)

APPOGGIATURA AND MORDENT (*Accent und Mordant,
Pincé et Port de Voix*): Frequently an appoggiatura is
followed by a mordent (Ex. 5). The single elements
of the combination follow the usual rules and exceptions.

Ex. 5 (Türk [1802], p. 309)

TURN (*Doppelschlag, Cadence, Double*): (Exs. 6,
7.) C. P. E. Bach (Chap. II, Sect. 4, Par. 20) distinguishes the turn from the ending of the trill with
termination, in remarking that the first notes of the
turn are played more quickly than the last, leaving a
slight pause on the last note, whereas the last notes of
the terminated trill always connect smoothly with the
following notes. For various tempi he gives corresponding versions.

Ex. 6 (C. P. E. B., Tab. V, Fig. L)

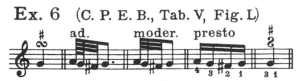

When the sign appears after the note, the execution is as follows:

Ex. 7 (C. P. E. B., Tab. V, Fig. LX, c 2)

These interpretations must be distinguished from that of the modern turn

Ex. 8 (R. L. K.)

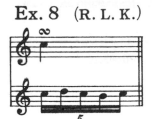

indicated thus by C. P. E. Bach:

Ex. 9 (C. P. E. B., Tab. V, Fig. LXIXa, b)

SLIDE (*Schleifer, Coulé*): The slide is indicated in Bach by the sign ⁀ or by small notes, and executed thus:

Ex. 10 (Marpurg, Tab. IV, Fig. 15)

In Ex. 11, we find another kind of slide used in chords to fill in thirds.

Ex. 11 (D'Anglebert)

Coulé sur une tierce

TRILL (*Triller, Tremblement*): It cannot be too emphatically stated that the Bach trill *always begins with the upper note*, in accordance with the nearly unanimous directions of eighteenth-century instruction books[8]. It is almost incredible that the nineteenth-century change to the modern practice of beginning on the lower note should have led people even to deliberate falsification of eighteenth-century texts like that in certain editions of Bach's own table of ornaments. Moreover it is rather disheartening nearly always to hear trills and other ornaments wrongly performed even by the best musicians of today. But quite inexcusable is the work of certain musicologists who have presumably worked for years with books like C. P. E. Bach's "Versuch" with its explicit directions, and yet make editions in which ornaments are written out as wrongly as if no evidence of eighteenth-century practice had survived. Perhaps the most flagrant example of such work (cited to augment the reader's caution against editorial misdeeds) is the edition by one of the foremost English musicologists of the Preludes from Couperin's "L'Art de Toucher le Clavecin". Here, in the face of Couperin's own table of ornaments and his own instructions in the very same book, are the most incredibly false realizations of signs so employed by Couperin as to leave no room for error.

The trill is indicated by the signs ⁀ or ⁀⁀ or *tr* or sometimes by a cross.

Ex. 12 (Marpurg, Tab. IV, Fig. 25)

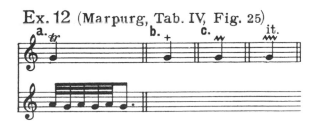

---

[8]The few exceptions to this practice seem to have no bearing on the work before us, and certainly have not been taken into account by the people who realize trills from below. It is hoped that this controversial matter may be settled once and for all by the eventual publication of a tabulation of these exceptions and a general survey, now in process, of all sources of information concerning eighteenth-century practice.

It should be noticed that the eighteenth-century trill, beginning upon the upper auxiliary note, has an appoggiatura character in the accentuation of the dissonance which gives it quite a different sense from the modern trill, which begins on the lower main note and has only the weaker character of a changing note.

TRILL WITH TERMINATION (*Triller mit Nachschlag, Trillo und Mordant, Tremblement et pincé*) (Ex. 13): The signs ⋀⋁ and ⋀⌣ indicate trills with termination (*mit Nachschlag*). This termination can frequently be introduced by the player when it is not already indicated or written out.

Ex. 13a. (J. S. Bach)   Ex. 13b. (R. L. K.)

PREPARED TRILL (*Accent und Trillo, Tremblement appuyé*): The appoggiatura character is especially emphasized in the *tremblemeǹt appuyé*, indicated ⊩⋀⋀, (Ex. 14), or sometimes only implied as a freedom of the player.

Ex. 14 (D'Anglebert)

TRILLS WITH PREFIX, EITHER FROM ABOVE OR FROM BELOW (*Triller von Oben* or *Triller von Unten, Doppelt-Cadence, Cadence*): The signs ⌒⋀⋀ and ⌒⋁⋀⋀ indicate trills with prefixes respectively from above and from below.

Ex. 15 (D'Anglebert)

Ex. 16 (D'Anglebert)

TIED TRILL (*Accent and Trillo, Gebundener* or *Angeschlossener Triller, Tremblement lié*): If, in the case of a downward diatonic progression, the trill is connected by a slur with the preceding note, that note is not repeated, but is tied over as the first note of the trill.

Ex. 17 (Marpurg, Tab. IV, Figs. 30, 31)

In many cases this slur can be pre-supposed even when not indicated by the composer, except in works of composers like Couperin, who was absolutely precise about his indications, even on this point. But in the works of composers who are not thus precise or consistent, there are many cases where the slur should not be presupposed, because the character of phrasing and accentuation make it desirable to sound again the first note of the trill instead of tying it to the preceding note.

HALF TRILL (*Prall Triller*): The true *Prall Triller* is a form of *Tremblement lié*, played very fast and

Ex. 18 (C. P. E. B., Tab. IV, Fig. XLV)

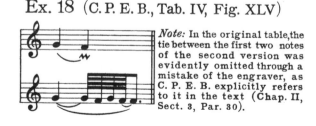

Note: In the original table, the tie between the first two notes of the second version was evidently omitted through a mistake of the engraver, as C. P. E. B. explicitly refers to it in the text (Chap. II, Sect. 3, Par. 30).

short, consisting, as Marpurg remarks (Anweisung [1755], Page 56, Note 2) of only three notes. It occurs in fast passages, or in slow movements just at the end of a long sustained appoggiatura, but in any case only following a downward stepwise progression (C. P. E. Bach, Chap. II, Sect. 3, Par. 34).

The inverted mordent (Ex. 19), now sometimes wrongly called *Prall Triller*, is never indicated by the trill sign, ∿, but is always written out in small notes and called a *Schneller*. Unlike the *Prall Triller*, the Schneller is not restricted to preparation by a downward stepwise progression, but can occur on quite separated notes.

Ex. 19 (Marpurg, Tab. V, Figs. 15, 16)

THE EXECUTION OF TRILLS

The rhythmic shape and number of beats in trills is variable. Couperin ("L'Art de Toucher le Clavecin") makes the following remarks:

"Although the trills are marked equal in the table of ornaments of my first book, they should nevertheless begin more slowly than they end, but this gradation should be imperceptible.

"Trills of any considerable length contain three elements, which in performance appear to be completely unified: 1. The leaning (*appuy*) upon the upper note. 2. The beats. 3. The stopping point.

Ex. 20 (Couperin, "L'Art de toucher le clavecin")

"As for other Trills, they are arbitrary. There are those which are prepared (*appuyé*) and others so short that they show neither preparation nor stopping point. One can even aspirate them." (See Var. 16, Bar 15 for a *tremblement aspiré*.)

Saint Lambert says ("Les Principes du Clavecin", Chap. 21): "When the trill must be long, it is more beautiful to beat it slowly at first and not to hurry it until the end; but when it is short it should always be prompt."

Here in the Variations, as well as elsewhere, distinctions should be made among:

1. Trills used as accents, especially on short notes, or leaving clear a rather large proportion of the main note. These are quickly disposed of and contain rather few "beats". (Var. 7, Bar 2, etc.; Var. 5, Bar 20, etc.)

2. Trills which are not accented but incorporated smoothly into the melodic line. These are played evenly and connected smoothly with the following notes. Such smooth trills frequently have terminations. (Var. 9, Bar 12, etc.; Var. 10, Bar 4.)

3. Trills which begin with an emphasis of their appoggiatura character, or a certain lingering on the upper note, like the *tremblement appuyé*. (Var. 21, Bar 6.)

4. Long trills. Such a trill becomes faster toward the middle and often slightly slower to round off the ending and to connect it smoothly with what follows. (Var. 22, bars 11, 12.) This is also frequently true of trills of any considerable length which have terminations. (Aria, Bar 3.)

5 Trills, most frequently on dotted notes or preceding tied-over notes or rests, which increase greatly in speed and end in a kind of snap just before the dot, tied note, or rest, as the case may be. (Var. 11, Bar 5, first version, etc.; Var. 13, Bar 12.) This snap is called *Schnellen* by C. P. E. Bach, and is described in connection with the *Prall Triller* (Chap. II, Sect. 3, Par. 32) and with the last beats of an accelerated trill (*Ibid.*, Par. 8). Sometimes it is followed by a rest in the place of the dot, making a *tremblement aspiré*. (Var. 16, Bar 15.)

*   *   *

Notes Concerning the Execution of the Ornaments in the Variations

The rhythmical values which are given to the written-out trills reproduce the fundamental characteristics of my present execution, but can undoubtedly well be subjected to alteration by myself as well as others. At any rate they give some indication of the frequently ignored but necessary shapeliness and expressive subtlety which should be given to all eighteenth-century ornamentation in accordance with its context. It has seemed useless to complicate the text with any indication of the fluctuating details of rhythmic freedom, which must necessarily be the result of the performer's own feeling. On the piano the trills could often be executed with fewer "beats". Certain trills may be given terminations where they are not indicated, but the versions given have been considered preferable.

The turns can often be given thus: ♪♪♪ , according to C. P. E. Bach's indications; but many of them can just as well be played smoothly: ♪♪♪♪ , etc.

ARIA:

Bar 2: The two appoggiaturas are interpreted by Dolmetsch as "*Nachschläge*" on the authority of Quantz (Chap. VIII, Par. 6), but it would seem that the rhythm and the sentiment demand appoggiaturas. One may play the first appoggiatura shorter than its written-out value. If the second appoggiatura were played long, according to rule, the two D's together would sound too hard on the harpsichord and give a false accent. See Bars 6 and 25.

Bar 4: Here a long appoggiatura following the rule would produce an ugly fourth between A and D.

Bar 6: See Bar 2.

Bar 7: The harmony would be less pure in this alternative version with the appoggiatura as an eighth-note, following an example of C. P. E. Bach ("Versuch", Chap. II, Sect. 2, Par. 11), (Ex. 21b.)

Ex. 21 (C. P. E. B., Tab. III, Fig. VI)

Bar 11: J. S. Bach seldom makes a distinction between the sign of the arpeggio upwards and that of the arpeggio downwards. This chord might also be broken upwards.

Bar 12: As in Bar 2 the first appoggiatura might also be very short. In Anna Magdalena Bach's note-book of 1725 only an appoggiatura D occurs, instead

of the *tremblement appuyé*. A termination may be added here.

Bar 14: The consonance of G, B, and D, and also the rhythm, would sound quite flat if the appoggiatura were played long. It can be played shorter than indicated.

Bar 16: The first appoggiatura may also be played as an eighth-note, according to an example of C. P. E. Bach similar to that referred to at Bar 7 (Ex. 21a). The octave D's of the third beat, unlike those in Bar 2, have an agreeable finality, and on the nuanceless harpsichord the octave following parallel motion gives the illusion of a *diminuendo* rather than the effect of accent which seems to occur after the contrary motion of Bar 2. See Bar 24.

Bar 18: The first two appoggiaturas may be played shorter.

Bar 19: Here again the accent of an octave on E would be unpleasant. In the second beat the resolution of the appoggiatura D sharp to E should still be connected with the harmony of C, even if the resolution coincides only with the passing note B. The result is a wonderful fluidity of harmony in which the trill on F sharp makes a delightful accent.

Bar 20: The sequence of fifths makes impossible a long appoggiatura resolving according to rule.

Bar 21: The appoggiatura must be short to prevent consecutive sevenths with the tenor.

Bar 22: It might have been consistent with the practice of C. P. E. Bach ("Versuch", Chap. II, Sect. 2, Par. 11; Ex. 21a), to prolong the appoggiatura the length of the entire quarter-note, were it not for the weakness of the resulting harmony. Obviously the resolution coinciding with the tenor F sharp would be undesirable.

Bar 24: The resolution of the first appoggiatura according to rule would be obviously impossible.

Bar 25: See Bar 2.

Bar 26: Here the octave G—G would be less disturbing, but consistency demands the present execution. The appoggiatura in the left hand might be played shorter.

VARIATION 5:

Bar 20: Here the weakness of the D sharp resolution is best expressed by an accelerated *tremblement lié*, instead of the renewed accent of an ordinary trill. This must occupy an almost imperceptible part of the note. Notice the contrasting accentual interpretation of the trill on G.

VARIATION 7:

Bar 2: Here the trills have almost the same crisp accentual effect as the mordents, and should occupy no more of the time of the main notes.

Bar 16: Here the customary practice is followed in connection with tied dotted notes (Quantz VIII, 9),

Ex. 22 (Quantz, Tab. VI, Figs. 15, 16)

but in Bar 8 harmonic purity demands the execution given.

VARIATION 8:

Bar 24: C. P. E. Bach gives an example of a similar case and its execution. (Ex. 21a.) Thus this appoggiatura might be played as a quarter-note.

VARIATION 9:

Bar 12: The imitation, of course, will follow the first voice exactly.

VARIATION 11:

Bar 5, etc.: These trills must end with a vigorous snap.

VARIATION 12:

Bar 4, 5: The trill is interpreted as a *tremblement lié* in order that the following mordent may imitate it in contrary motion. These may also be played respectively as simple Prall Triller and short mordent.

Bars 29, 30: Here likewise the mordent imitates the trill in contrary motion.

VARIATION 13:

Bar 2: C. P. E. Bach writes ("Versuch", Chap. II, Section 2, Par. 14): "When the appoggiatura sounds the octave of the bass, it cannot be long, because the harmony would sound too empty".

Bar 6: Here the dissonant resolution of the appoggiatura gives an extraordinary savour to the harmony.

VARIATION 15:

Bars 7, 8: See notes to Variation 12, Bars 4, 5 or 29, 30.

VARIATION 16:

The inexact indication of dotted notes in eighteenth-century music is mentioned in the books of C. P. E. Bach, Quantz, Agricola ("Anleitung zur Singkunst", 1757)[9], and Leopold Mozart ("Versuch einer gründlichen Violinschule", 1756).

C. P. E. Bach says (Chap. 3, Par. 23): "The short notes following dots will always be dispatched as shorter than the notation indicates, thus it is superfluous to define these short notes by the use of dots or strokes." "In Ex. 23 we see their expression.

Ex. 23 (C. P. E. B., Tab. VI, Fig. VII)

At times the arrangement of parts (Eintheilung) demands that one proceed according to their literal notation * (*Schreibart*)." "The dots after short notes, followed by notes still shorter, should be held out."

Ex. 24 (C. P. E. B., Tab. VI, Fig. VIII)

The following passage in Agricola (p. 133), is quoted by Dannreuther (Vol. I, p. 191). "Short notes which follow dots, especially sixteenth- and thirty-second notes, and in *alla breve* time, ¢, $\frac{2}{2}$, even eighth-notes, are invariably taken very short—the notes preceding the dots being held so much the longer."

[9]An amplified translation of Pier Francesco Tosi: *Opinioni de' Cantori antichi e moderni, o sieno osservazioni sopra il Canto figurato*. Bologna. 1723.

Quantz writes (Chap. V. Par. 21): "In the case of dotted eighth-, sixteenth-, and thirty-second-notes, one departs from the general rule, because of the vivacity which they should express. It must be noticed, above all, that the note following the dot in Ex. 25a and b, should be played as quickly as that in Ex. 25c, whether in slow or fast tempo. Whence it follows that the dotted notes in Ex. 25a demand nearly the whole time of a quarter-note, and those in Ex. 25b nearly that of an eighth-note. One cannot exactly determine the time of the short note following the dot."

Ex. 25 (Quantz, Tab. II, Fig. 7, c, d, e)

(Chap. XVII, Sect. 2, Par. 16): "When thirty-second-notes follow a long note and a short rest (Ex. 26) they should always be played very quickly, whether in an *Adagio* or in an *Allegro*. Hence, to avoid faulty time, one must wait to the very end of the allotted time before playing them.

Ex. 26 (Quantz, Tab. XXII, Fig. 29)

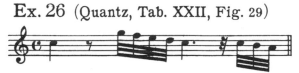

"If in a slow *alla breve* or in ordinary common time there is a sixteenth-rest on the down-beat followed by dotted notes (Exs. 27 a, b), the rest must be played as if there were either a dot or a pause of half the value following it, and as if the following notes were twice as short." (In other words, like Ex. 27, aa, bb).

Ex. 27 (Quantz, Tab. XXII, Figs. 30, 31)

(Chap. XVII, Sect. 7, Par. 58): "Moreover, in this measure ¢ , as well as in 3-4 time, which one

employs for the Loure, the Sarabande, the Courante, and the Chaconne, the eighth-notes following dotted quarters are not expressed according to their proper value, but shortly and sharply. The dotted note is emphasized and the bow is detached during the dot. One does likewise with all dotted notes if the time permits, and when there are three or more thirty-second notes after a dot or a rest, they are not executed according to their real value, especially in slow pieces; but, awaiting the very end of the time allotted them, one plays them then with the utmost speed, as is often the case in Ouvertures, Entrées and Furies. However one must give a separate bowing to each of these quick notes, and one can hardly slur anything."

This last is an excellent description of the vigorous *détaché* style in which the Ouverture (Variation 16) should be played.

Although these quotations explain the inaccurate notation and the true execution of much eighteenth-century music, especially the slow sections of French Ouvertures (and one must at all times bear them in mind), in much music of Bach there is still some room for doubt as to whether ♩. ♪ occurring against ♫ ♫ should be taken ♩ ♫ . In many cases, also here, one can be influenced alternately by Bach's obviously mere orthographical convention of writing ♩. ♪ instead of ♩ ♫ in *alla breve* time, and by passages where he definitely intended the literal interpretation of ♩. ♪ and ♫ ♫ , such as those in the "Kunst der Fuge" and the "Musikalisches Opfer" where dotted themes appear simultaneously in augmentation and in their natural form. Here, after having for some time played as sixteenths the eighths following dotted quarters, I have finally decided, at least for the present, upon their literal interpretation, especially as the sound of the harpsichord is given greater continuity through the increased complexity of rhythmic motion. I actually play the sixteenths shorter than noted, and undertook at first to write them out thus: ♫ , but was dissuaded by what seemed unnecessary complication of the text. Likewise there is here no attempt to indicate the rests (implied by Quantz above in speaking of the detached bow) which can take the place of the dots.

Bars 4, 5: A termination may be added here. In fact Marpurg says (Anweisung, [1755], Page 57, Note 4) that such "prepared trills" are always given a termination. One may question whether such a rule was the result of unanimous contemporary opinion, as it is not mentioned by C. P. E. Bach, or Türk, or indicated in D'Anglebert's table. At any rate the remaining "prepared trills" in this variation do not require the addition of a termination where not indicated, since the function of the termination is already performed by the succeeding quick notes (as C. P. E. Bach points out in parallel passages [Chap. II, Sect. III, Par. 16]).

Bar 28: The version with a "Triller von unten" is given to avoid the fifths resulting from the literal interpretation of the original, which might offend a fastidious ear.

Bars 31, 33: Here likewise especial care has been taken in shortening the termination of the trill to avoid the fifths which would otherwise occur.

VARIATION 22:

Bar 11: This trill should be incorporated smoothly in the melodic line and played as rhythmically independent from the bass, with a slight speeding up in the middle and slowing off toward the end. It is useless to attempt to indicate the exact number of "beats".

VARIATION 23:

Bar 23: Best as a Prall Triller. The trill should take as little of the time of the main note as possible.

VARIATION 24:

Bar 17: A rough attempt has been made to indicate the changes of speed without specifying the number of "beats" in the middle portion.

VARIATION 25:

Bar 13: The appoggiatura on the second beat is found written out by Bach in the corresponding place in Bars 21 and 22. Although this same appoggiatura has been introduced in the first two bars, in other corresponding places further use of it is left to the taste of the player.

VARIATION 26:

See notes to Variation 16 for information concerning the indeterminate value of dotted notes in eighteenth-century notation. See also following note.

VARIATION 29:

(See also Notes to Variation 16). Marpurg ("Anleitung" [1755], P. 24) makes the following remarks:

"It is frequently customary to employ simultaneously a simple and a composite measure, for example 12-8 against ₵ (Ex. 28a, b) as well as 6-8 against 2-4, or 9-8 against 3-4, and so forth. If in this combination of measures two notes of equal value occur against three others likewise of equal value, for example, two eighth-notes against three other eighth-notes, or two quarter-notes against three others, the first two of the three equal notes will always be played against the first of the two. Thus, for instance, those in Ex. 28a will all be played as in Ex. 28c, and even if the first of the two equal notes is dotted (Ex. 28b), they must nevertheless be played as in Ex. 28c. The so-called triplets which one uses in simple measures have their origin in this mixture of measures. These are such that one takes three eighths against a quarter, three sixteenths against an eighth, etc."

Ex. 28 (Marpurg, Tab. I, Figs. 42, 43)

VARIATION 30:

Bar 2: A *tremblement lié* seems best.

V

FINGERING

In playing Bach it seems best to use a frankly modern fingering based upon the now traditional succession of five fingers and crossing thumb. Thus fingers rarely cross, except in polyphonic passages, where there is often occasion to change fingers on the same note to ensure *legato*. A compromise is advisable between the old principle of avoiding the use of the thumb on "black" keys and that of avoiding changes of five-finger position or using similar fingering for sequential repetitions of figures. All jumps of position and breaks of *legato* can be fitted to places where they can automatically determine the phrasing. Thus the *legato* is always protracted wherever desired throughout the duration of the phrase.

With these conceptions in mind it is rather difficult to understand some eighteenth-century fingering as represented in Bach's own indications (Bachgesellschaft edition, Volume 36, Pages 224, 225, 237, 126), or in the sonatas of C. P. E. Bach's "Versuch über die wahre Art das Clavier zu spielen". Here one finds detached fingering which makes it almost impossible to play passages altogether smoothly which we would feel to require *legato* playing. Is this detached style entirely intentional? Or is it a compromise brought about by the traditions of a technic just beginning to cultivate a certain equality of the five fingers and a substitution of the modern crossing under of the thumb for the old principle of passing a longer finger over a shorter one (C major scale, right hand: 1 2 3 4 3 4 3 4 etc.)?

In playing the pieces of Couperin, one should follow faithfully Couperin's own fingering or his principles, for there the fingering seems absolutely essential to the phrasing, to such a degree is the piece conceived idiomatically in terms of the keyboard and of the hand. But with Bach, whose clavier music is so much less idiomatic, and often inspired by other instruments, one constantly feels the necessity of bringing to the keyboard the smoothness and suppleness of string or voice phrasing.

VI

PHRASING

It is perhaps significant that in eighteenth-century treatises one never finds specific talk of "phrasing", for it is lumped together with musical feeling and harmonic and melodic sensitiveness. C. P. E. Bach relegates it to the chapter "Vom Vortrage" where he remarks (Chap. 3, Par. 8), in the course of saying really discouragingly little: "To obtain an insight into the real content and sentiment of a piece, and, in the absence of the necessary signs, to judge the notes in it, whether they should be played *legato* or *staccato*, as well as what must be considered regarding the introduction of ornaments, one would do well to obtain the opportunity of hearing soloists as well as groups of players".

(Chap. 3, Par. 12.) "Here we must add that especially one should miss no chance to hear good singers. Through this one learns to think in terms of singing, and will do well thereafter to sing a phrase to oneself in order to hit upon its proper rendering."

But how seldom nowadays do we hear good Bach phrasing, and least of all from singers! Because singing alone cannot help us, although it is one of the surest ways of determining proper phrasing, and because, alas, the concert hall can give us little good instruction, we must try to discover for ourselves the elements of Bach phrasing with a more orderly and analytical approach than that of C. P. E. Bach and other happy musicians who had less need of theorizing.

In arriving at something rather like C. P. E. Bach's definition of "Vortrag", we might define phrasing as the exposition through dynamic and agogic means of the relationship, relative value, and expressiveness of the notes composing a melodic line or a harmonic section. In the music of Bach, which is formally so highly organized, these relationships are particularly subtle and complicated. We must know how and where to divide and connect the notes into groups, and where and how these small groups are contained in larger groups. Within each group we must know what is the relative importance of the notes, beyond the constant rhythmic relation of strong and weak beats; which are the notes of introduction, of climax, and of conclusion in a melodic phrase; as well as which are the notes of harmonic importance and those of importance in the main melodic and harmonic progressions of sections and of the whole piece.

The performer's task in converting a piece into sound is like that of a painter who must understand thoroughly the anatomy of his model and the relation of the smallest detail to the whole, not so much that the original may be faithfully reproduced as that his own feeling about it and his choice of technical means for its interpretation may be controlled by the complete inner logic of nature. Thus here in the music of Bach we are confronted with the task of making clear the articulation and poetic significance of complicated structures which rival those of nature in their obedience to all her inner laws of balance, of proportion, of form.

One of the most important and practically least recognized characteristics of Bach's music is the fusion of form and expression almost to the point of identification. Thus, the musical feeling leading to the true expression of a Bach phrase can frequently be guided largely by the intellect—and often must be, until the musical perceptions reach a degree of instinctive sharpness not so often demanded by other music.

Although "phrasing" involves a consideration of the music in many phases and from many points of view, here on paper we can only attempt to isolate and discuss the most important elements and to make a number of perhaps rash generalizations.

First, and for us here most important, is the consideration of individual voices as single melodic lines, ignoring for the time being their relationship to each other.

The fundamental rule which underlies of course all measured music is the rhythmic relation of weak beats to strong beats, and the different functions of the first, second, third, and fourth beats.

Weak beats generally tend to be connected with the following strong beat, so that most pauses are likely to occur after strong beats. However, this very rough generalization must not allow us to ignore the musical parallel of feminine endings in verse. It

seems to me that many writers, even including Schweitzer, to whom we owe so much, have over-emphasized the progression from the weak to the strong beat—in other words, iambic movement at the expense of trochaic movement. In many fast movements, such as those of the concertos, this trochaic movement, by its very holding back, gives the impression of tremendous energy pulsing under the harness of superhuman restraint. Likewise it seems to me that in many Bach phrases there are quite as many subsidiary notes which take their rhythmic momentum from a preceding strong note like the successive bounces of a thrown or dropped tennis ball, as there are those which progress forward to a strong beat like a ball rolling down a slope. And there are notes which perform a double function, in relation to both preceding and succeeding strong beats. In many Bach performances one hears either the flabbiness of rolling or the excessive jumpiness of bouncing, for lack of balance between the two kinds of motion. The parallel in dancing is easily perceptible. Exs. 33-39 show a few of many possible modes of rhythmic thought which can work together to produce the equilibrium.

Syncopated notes, or notes tying over a strong beat, often have a peculiar character, being approached with a certain spring or sighing effect, the impulse coming from the preceding strong beat. Leopold Mozart says ("Versuch einer gründlichen Violinschule" [Chap. I, Sect. 3, Par. 18, Note k]): "Such notes must be attacked strongly and held with a gradually diminishing quietness (*eine nach und nach verlierende Stille*) without renewed pressure, like the gradually disappearing sound of a sharply struck bell."

The melodic determination of note-grouping, even in the face of so many complicated and intangible elements, permits a few crude generalizations. Notes moving stepwise are more often played *legato* in contrast to the detached *staccato* performance of jumping notes. (We might make an exception to this remark in the case of notes outlining arpeggiated harmony in quick time.) Likewise, an interruption of stepwise progression by a leap of the melodic line often requires a phrasing corresponding to the necessary vocal rendition or to the parallel sensation of bodily movement. However, one must not take these principles too seriously, in view of thousands of instances where they are superseded by more important factors.

For nearly all the keyboard music of Bach it is extremely illuminating to think in terms of string bowing. Thus one can often determine the divisions of sequential figures and stepwise passages, also the texture of *legato* and of relative degrees of *staccato*. Between thinking of string bowing and feeling the instinctive vocal inflection (as recommended by C. P. E. Bach) one is fairly sure to arrive at a natural phrasing. Vocal inflection itself (except in the case of singers, as I am inclined maliciously to remark), is closely governed by mysterious laws of kinæsthetic feeling and of bodily movement. For example, a phrase or movement can often be explained in terms of springing, falling, or bouncing.

The phrasing must make clear the main progressions underlying more or less elaborate decoration of the melodic line. Often in Bach, especially in two-voice pieces, a single voice will outline harmonies and carry on in broken form the progressions of two- or three-part harmony. This of course must be understood by the player and expressed by the phrasing.

Ex. 33 (Var. 5, Bar 13)

etc.

The exposition of the manifold melodic, harmonic, and rhythmic implications of many such single voice passages demands absolute balance of rhythm. Such is the foregoing example, whose richness depends

upon a superposition in the finished performance of the various phases which are shown separately here.

An example like this, with its many parallels, goes to demonstrate the fact that much Bach phrasing exists far more in time, that is in living rhythmic patterns, than in the spatial articulation and exaggerated nuancing of melodic figures usually emphasized by Bach performers (more unfortunately, for example, in the unaccompanied violin sonatas) at the expense of the rhythmic vitality and organic unity of the whole. In fact, one is sometimes led to feel that the cumulative effect of sharply defined rhythmic detail incorporated into a steady pulse is far more important in many Bach movements than the inflections of tone and dynamics; and even that some of the Bach sonatas could be given a performance on a drum which would be far more thrilling than that of most string players. Of course the ideal performance does justice to both elements. In other words, the music cannot become fully alive in a performance which develops plastic shape by heightening melodic contours through light and shade of dynamics and variation of *staccato* and *legato* texture, yet fails to endow these shapes with their own rhythmic form carved out of precise time-divisions, just as they are carved so to speak, out of pitch, and dynamic intensity, in perfectly proportioned relation to the whole. Anything else resembles the blurred, lopsided contours of sculpture in wax beginning to melt under the hot sun.

Even had the preceding topic of the grouping of notes into phrases been properly treated, one would still need to make a large book to explain the relationships of notes within these phrases, a thing which we can hardly expect more than to suggest here. So far we have spoken principally of the smaller groups of notes more in the sense of texture than in the sense of phrases which make small entities in themselves and which in turn go to build up a larger unit. These phrases have a definite plastic form, to which the sense and perceptions must be sharpened in recognizing the functions of every note, whether it be as introduction, climax, conclusion, coda, or mere decoration.

When we begin to put the voices together, the resulting harmony has an influence, especially on the phrasing of the longer sections. The building up of a stress or tension resolving to repose, although it occurs melodically, we find especially in harmonic progressions and in the relation of dissonance and consonance. Here we are not so much obliged to grapple with this difficult subject, because the Variations are all built on the same fundamental harmony and on the same rhythmic skeleton of four eight-bar phrases, much as they sometimes stretch these bounds.

Another important feature, when all the voices are put together, is the texture of the whole. It must not be too close, but must have air, so to speak. On the other hand, especially on the harpsichord, one must not break it apart with ''holes'' caused by too short or misplaced *staccato*. This can occur most easily when the bass is played too short, thus removing the bottom of the structure too suddenly. The distribution of *legato* and *staccato* must balance through the whole counterpoint, like the distribution of black and white in a well made woodcut.

I might remark, in connection with harpsichord phrasing, that the principal means of distinguishing notes consists in infinitely varying degrees of *legato* and *staccato* (although the instrument is to some extent capable of accent) and, through the use of these very means of *legato* and *staccato*, of the illusion of slight nuance. On the harpsichord one must guard against making too short *staccato*, as the effect is quite unlike that of the piano, in that the plucked string must be given sufficient time to vibrate, whereas the struck string vibrates instantly in pure sound.

Perhaps these remarks, for all their inadequacy, will demonstrate the futility of attempting at all to indicate phrasing in the text, and perhaps they will convey some idea of the way in which the player must separate and analyze every phrase of these Variations, the function of every note within that phrase, and the organization of smaller phrases into larger ones, and finally into the whole.

VII

TEMPO

In the table on p. xxvi are indicated tempi used in performing the Variations. These may vary, however, according to the instrument and acoustical conditions, and of course according to the phrasing chosen—even, I fear, according to the metronome! The tempo should be maintained very strictly within each variation.

In Bach, especially in strongly rhythmical fast movements, clarity and coherence demand a degree of precision in the small note-values which is less frequently necessitated by other music, where complete rhythmic exactitude is often left only to the main beats.

This rhythmic precision is especially necessary to performance on a nuanceless instrument like the organ or the harpsichord, where the weakening effect of most rhythmic freedom cannot be compensated by nuance. On the clavichord, for example, one can play the same pieces much less strictly than on the harpsichord, because any rhythmic flexibility may be combined with a complete flexibility of nuance to produce something warm and perfectly human, whereas on the harpsichord or organ such freedom,

going only half way, cannot have the same sincerity of effect.

For slow movements we should make some exception to the above remarks, because there the expression frequently depends upon a certain flexibility of small notes within the frame of the main beats. However, one of the greatest dangers in *tempo rubato* is that slight rhythmic fluctuations which were originally sincere and inspired by perfect taste, in the course of the successive imitations which a professional performer is likely to make of his first good conception and performance become mannered and exaggerated, having lost some of their original significance, resembling the affected movements of a bad dancer.

Moreover, in most Bach movements, all harmonic and melodic detail is arranged in such a symmetrical relation to the whole phrase or movement that the musical structure can often be distorted by rhythmical fluctuations, like an elaborate Baroque facade mirrored in troubled water,—or, as one is inclined to say in reminiscence of some performances, thrown helter skelter by a series of earthquakes!

In contrast to the fluid legato of the canons and slow movements, the fast variations, especially those for two keyboards, should have a kind of sparkling precision, down to the smallest note values. It is very beneficial to practise these fast variations with a metronome, and wise even thus to test the accuracy of larger rhythmical values in the slow movements, in order to insure against unconscious extremes of *rubato*.

Of course there are two ways of achieving a true accuracy of rhythm and tempo, a quality which for the most part is not natural to the human organism of changing pulse rates. For just as one can fall below the human level into an insensitive and mechanical kind of metronomical strictness (some of the most unrhythmical playing in the world comes from persons practising with a metronome), so one can rise above the weakness of vacillating flesh and blood to an unswerving rhythmic strength and inevitability which, associated with balanced, sensitive phrasing, can only be described as supernatural.

The metronome is only a mechanical means of assistance and can in no way take the place of a real feeling for tempo, which is a constant inner sense of the rhythmical relationship of each part to the whole. The acquisition of such a sense of tempo may be aided in practice by singing a rhythmic motive from one part of a piece while playing another. Attention is called here to some of the useful and enlightening patterns or modes of rhythmic thought that are to be found among the inexhaustible riches of these variations (Exs. 33-39). These all suggest modes of obtaining from smaller note-values a rhythmic precision controlled by musical feeling rather than imposed only by mechanical finger discipline.

Ex.34 (Var. 8, Bar 11)

etc.

Ex.35 (Var. 26, Bar 9)

etc.

Ex.36 (Var. 14, Bar 1)

etc.

Ex. 37 (Var. 28, Bar 1)

Ex. 38 (Var. 17, Bars 21-22)

Ex. 39 (Var. 20, Bar 9)

Similarly in the Aria one may sing the rhythm of the first eight bars against the last eight, in bass as well as soprano, or superpose the sixteenth- or the eighth-note motion of the last bars on any preceding section of the Aria. Or one may sing simply the bass, either in its simplest form (dotted half-notes) or in a figure of quarter-notes. Especially useful in establishing rhythmic equilibrium is playing the movement through alternately thinking in ♩ ♩. ♪, the characteristic sarabande movement, or ♩. ♪♩, or even occasionally ♫ ♩. If one becomes thus sensitive to the many simultaneous rhythmic pulses, from sixteenth-notes to whole beats, or the rhythmic relation of measures within a phrase, one begins to understand part of the real vitality of most Bach movements.

In Var. 8, this figure ♫♫ ♩ ♫♫ from the beginning, may be used to keep the left hand under control from bars 9 to 16.

In Var. 11, this figure, ♩. ♩ ♩ may be superposed on bars 27 to 32.

In Var. 13, an alternation between ♫ ♩ or ♫. ♩ and ♩. ♫♫ may be useful.

In Var. 14, the performer in playing the opening passage should be mindful of the subsequent thirty-second note rhythm. The last two bars should be heard both in sixteenth-notes and in thirty-seconds.

In Var. 17, the rhythm ♩. ♫ is very helpful, as well as the whole figure ♬♬ ♩.♫ ♬♬ against ♬♬♬ or ♩ ♩ ♩.

In Var. 20, the triplet rhythm should be superposed on the rhythm of the opening section.

In Var. 26, ♪| ♫.♫♫ ♩ ♪| etc., is the key to the whole movement.

In Var. 28, the eighth-note motion should always be felt. The trills will be smooth if they are always felt simultaneously as coming from the impulse of the preceding strong beat and joining smoothly with the following.

THE GOLDBERG VARIATIONS

Registration*		Tempo†	
ARIA	I 8'	♩ = 56	(62)
Variatio 1. a 1 Clav.	8' 4'	♩ = 94	(95)
Variatio 2. a 1 Clav.	16' 4'	♩ = 56	(63)
Variatio 3. Canone all' Unisono, a 1 Clav.	I 8'	♩. = 40	(46)
Variatio 4. a 1 Clav.	II 8' 4' Lute	♪ = 156	(♩. = 56)
Variatio 5. a 1 overo 2 Clav.	I 8', II 8'	♩ = 126	(132)
Variatio 6. Canone alla Seconda, a 1 Clav.	I 8'	♪ = 132	(118)
Variatio 7. a 1 overo 2 Clav.	II 8' (piano)	♩. = 72	(74)
Variatio 8. a 2 Clav.	I 8', II 8'	♩ = 86	(92)
Variatio 9. Canone alla Terza, a 1 Clav.	I 8'	♩ = 58	(64)
Variatio 10. Fughetta, a 1 Clav.	I 8' II 8'	𝅗𝅥 = 80	(82)
Variatio 11. a 2 Clav.	I 8', II 8	♩. = 72	(82)
Variatio 12. Canone alla Quarta	I 8'	♩ = 66	(63)
Variatio 13. a 2 Clav.	4', 8' (Lute ?)	♩ = 40	(44)
Variatio 14. a 2 Clav.	I 8', II 8'	♩ = 80	(92)
Variatio 15. Canone alla Quinta, a 1 Clav.	I 8'	♪ = 54	(58)
Variatio 16. Ouverture, a 1 Clav.	16' I 8' II 8' 4'	♩ = 72, ♩. = 60 (♩ = 66, ♪ = 184)	
Variatio 17. a 2 Clav.	I 8', II 8'	♩ = 108	(116)
Variatio 18. Canone alla Sesta, a 1 Clav.	I 8'	𝅗𝅥 = 66	(71)
Variatio 19. a 1 Clav.	II 8' Lute	♪ = 152	(152)
Variatio 20. a 2 Clav.	I 8', II 8'	♩ = 86	(100)
Variatio 21. Canone alla Settima	I 8'	♩ = 56	(55)
Variatio 22. a 1 Clav. Alla breve	8' 4'	𝅗𝅥 = 76	(76)
Variatio 23. a 2 Clav.	I 8', II 8'	♩ = 102	(108)
Variatio 24. Canone all' Ottava, a 1 Clav.	I 8'	♩. = 56	(56)
Variatio 25. a 2 Clav.	4', 16' (Lute or 8' Lute?)	♪ = 46	(55)
Variatio 26. a 2 Clav.	I 8', II 8'	♩ = 84	(94)
Variatio 27. Canone alla Nona, a 2 Clav.	I 8', II 8'	♩. = 60	(69)
Variatio 28. a 2 Clav.	I 8', II 8'	♩ = 80	(88)
Variatio 29. a 1 overo 2 Clav.	16' I 8' II 8' 4'	♩ = 88	(94)
Variatio 30. a 1 Clav. Quodlibet	I 6' I 8' II 8' 4'	♩ = 80	(80)
ARIA da Capo	I 8'	♩ = 56	(62)

*Solo 16' or 4' should be used here in such a way as to sound at normal eight-foot pitch. "I" indicates the lower manual, "II" the upper. The presence of commas indicates the use of two keyboards. Otherwise the indication of stops from both upper and lower manuals implies the use of the coupler from the uppermanual to the lower. Allowance is made here both for instruments like the so-called Bach harpsichord with four-foot on the upper manual and for those with four-foot on the lower.

†The second set of metronome indications (in parentheses) was made eighteen months before the first. For the sake of truthfulness, both are given, strongly as I now repudiate some of the earlier tempi. Where the points of adjustment of the ordinary metronome did not seem satisfactory at the time of measurement, points in between are indicated.

VIII

DYNAMICS

A harpsichord registration is indicated in the table of tempi. It should be noticed that this registration is intended to enhance the symmetrical arrangement of the variations, in that the same 8' register is employed for all the canons and the same combination for all the two-manual arabesques, whereas the greatest possible variety is brought to the other assorted forms, in accordance with their character.

Changes of registration within the variations are quite uncalled-for; they only bring a kind of disturbing restlessness to the expression and utterly destroy the architectural symmetry. Each movement has its own tone-color, within which all the expressiveness of declamation and nuances of form can be brought out by touch and phrasing.

This same character should be preserved in a performance on the piano, by preserving a certain unity of volume and color within each variation and by employing the resources of nuance only in smaller degrees in order to enhance the declamation of individual phrases. One only does violence to the music by attempting to render the form of the whole movement into pianistic chiaroscuro. However, each variation should be given a distinctly characterized color or dynamic level. The pedal should of course be used very sparingly and only for coloring, not for sustaining, and should seldom be allowed to interfere with the written rhythmical values.

A false kind of expressiveness and emotional climacticism should not be imposed upon this music.

Neither must we react against nineteenth-century fashions in favor of a mechanical, rigidly shallow, "abstract" style of Bach playing.

As one must understand the difference between the heartrending ravings of a Philoctetes and the intellectual serenity of a Socrates in a Platonic dialogue like the Phaedo, though realizing that the human implications of the one are no greater than of the other; so one must distinguish in this music the elements which directly appeal to the senses and those which we would no more treat with the physical immediacy, one might almost say importunacy, of much of Wagner, than we would read a sonnet of Shakespeare with dramatic inflection and a break in our voices.

As has been too often forgotten, there is much in music that is nobler and emotionally more profound than superficial pathos of declamation—

"Thoughts that do often lie too deep for tears".

As far as expression through dynamics is concerned, here is an entirely different stuff from Beethoven or Wagner, a kind of music which within a movement undergoes very little change of sentiment or increase of intensity. The real expression depends upon the finest feeling for the significance of the fundamental, germinal phrases, inwardly sung melodies, intensely felt rhythmic figures and sensitive harmonic inflections; and the ability to expose, fully and nobly developed in objective clarity, the continuity and emotional logic of the whole.

IX

GENERAL INTERPRETATION

However much it is an act of impudence thus to discuss something which is far too profound and complex to be grasped in words, it seems necessary, in order to explain all that has been said before, to confess some of the feelings which inevitably come with the playing of this music.

The Aria seems to foreshadow the spirit of the whole work through the tenderness and calm with which the solemnity of the fundamental bass is clothed at its initial appearance.

The first variation stands like a festive gateway leading to the inner world exposed in the following three variations. These, like so many of the canons and the Aria, have an unearthly pure sweetness and a lyricism in every phrase that makes one long to dissolve one's fingers, the instrument, and one's whole self into three or four singing voices. For a moment this quiet lyricism is interrupted by the shining smooth swiftness of the first arabesque variation. Then comes a second canon of an almost nostalgic tenderness; then a faraway scherzo of the utmost lightness and delicacy. The following arabesque and canon return to a lyricism which is interrupted by the brusque roughness of the Fughetta. This is followed by the delicate network of the third arabesque and the sunny canon at the fourth. Then comes a flute aria of a breath-taking quiet pure joy. The humor of the fourth arabesque makes even more striking the appearance of the dark tragic canon at the fifth which ends the first half of the variations.

The second half opens with a majestic French Ouverture, followed by one of the lightest of the arabesque variations. In the sixth canon and the lute-variation we return to a lyric sweetness like that of the beginning, but more peaceful. Another scherzo arabesque contrasts with the sombre seventh canon, which in turn joins on to the *alla breve* variation. This, for all its quicker tempo, transforms the chromatic pathos of the canon into that kind of serene chastened joy which follows pain. In the seventh arabesque we burst forth in the most unrestrained exuberant joy, which is tranquilized in the gentle rocking of the canon at the octave. Again we are interrupted to be carried to even greater tragic heights on the waves of a quiet yet irresistibly passionate aria. From the eighth arabesque on, the variations mount through a sprightly canon, glittering trills, and waltz-like bravura to the final jubilant climax in the Quodlibet, upon which the repetition of the Aria falls like a benediction.

But for all their lyricism and tragic passion and exuberance, the Aria and the Variations seem of a divine substance entirely refined and purified of anything personal or ignoble, so that in playing them one seems only the unworthy mouthpiece of a higher voice. And even beyond the scope of the emotions that have been aroused, the effect of the whole is one of boundless peace, in which one returns cleansed, renewed, matured to the starting point, which seen a second time seems so transfigured in the light of this traversed spiritual journey.

But how Bach himself in pious humility would ridicule these high-sounding words of ours with a wry face and with god-like laughter:

"Kraut und Rüben. . . ."

RALPH KIRKPATRICK

Salzburg, September 15, 1934.

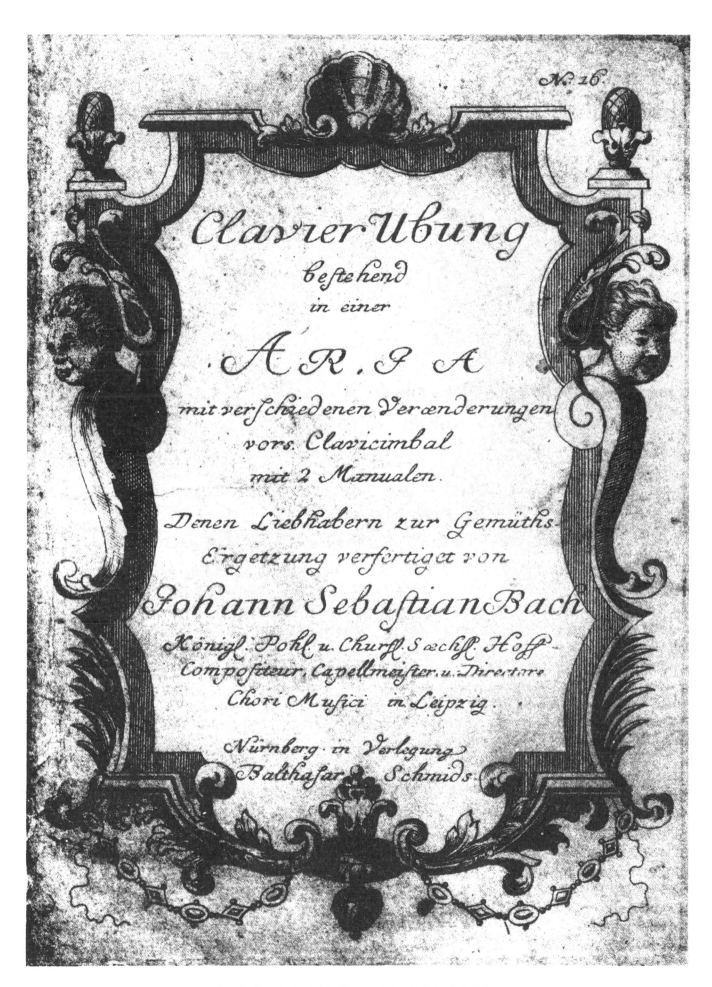

Clavier Ubung
bestehend
in einer
ARIA
mit verschiedenen Veränderungen
vors. Clavicimbal
mit 2 Manualen.

Denen Liebhabern zur Gemüths-
Ergetzung verfertiget von

Johann Sebastian Bach
Königl. Pohl. u. Churfl. Sæchß. Hoff-
Compositeur, Capellmeister u. Directore
Chori Musici in Leipzig.

Nürnberg in Verlegung
Balthasar Schmids.

Facsimile of the Title Page of the Original Edition

*"There is something in it of Divinity more than the ear dis-
covers: it is an Hieroglyphical and shadowed lesson of the
whole World, and creatures of God; such a melody to the ear, as
the whole World, well understood, would afford the understanding.   In brief, it is a sensible fit of that harmony which
intellectually sounds in the ears of God."*

Sir Thomas Browne: "Religio Medici" (1643)

Aria

(Execution of the Ornaments)

(Original Text)

28

32

6

8

Variatio 2 a 1 Clav.

*For a clearer view of the voice leading, the right hand part is set out on the two small staves, in this Variation and in Variations 3, 6 and 9.

Variatio 3   Canone all' Unisuono a 1 Clav.

Variatio 4 a 1 Clav.

Variatio 5 a 1 ovvero 2 Clav.

Variatio 6 Canone alla Seconda a 1 Clav.

Variatio 7 a 1 ovvero 2 Clav.

Variatio 8 a 2 Clav.

20

24

Variatio 9 Canone alla Terza a 1 Clav.

26

Variatio 10 Fughetta a 1 Clav.

Variatio **11** a 2 Clav.

Variatio 12 Canone alla Quarta

Variatio **13** a 2 Clav.

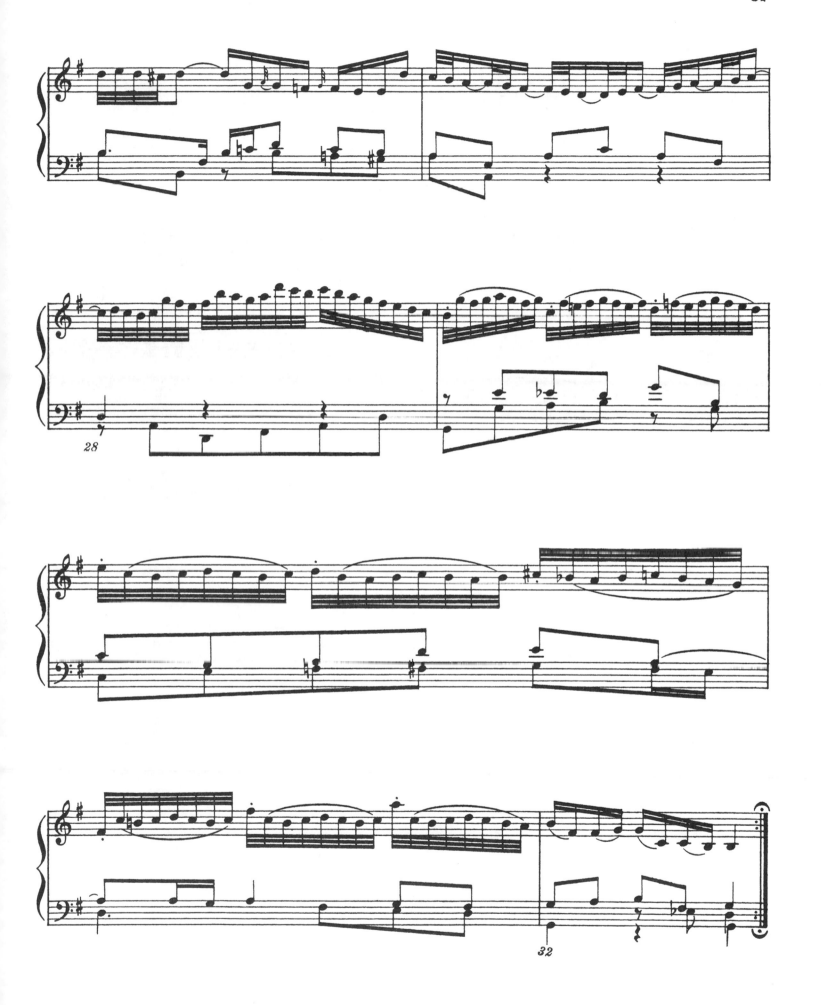

Variatio 14 a 2 Clav.

Variatio 15 Canone alla Quinta a 1 Clav.

Andante

Variatio 16 a 1 Clav **Ouverture**

48

Variatio **17** a **2** Clav.

Variatio 18 Canone alla Sesta a 1 Clav.

Variatio **19** a 1 Clav.

Variatio 20 a 2 Clav.

Variatio 21 Canone alla Settima

Variatio 22 a 1 Clav.
Alla breve

Variatio **23** a 2 Clav.

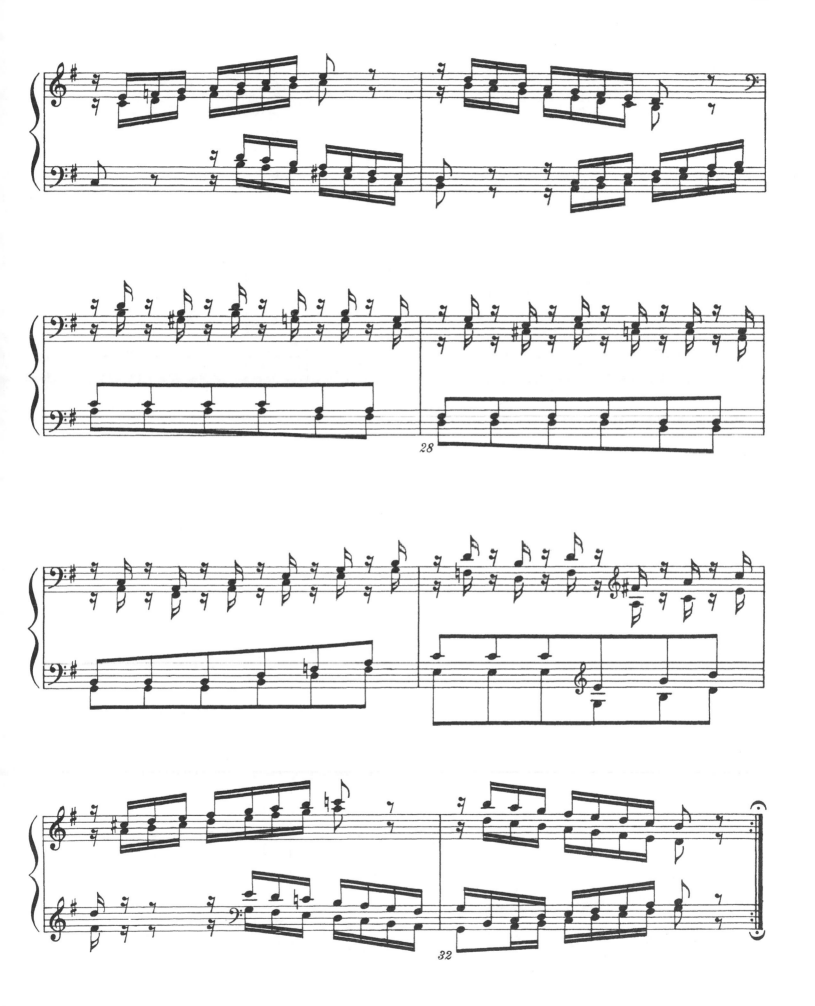

Variatio 24 Canone all'Ottava a1 Clav.

Variatio **26** a **2** Clav.

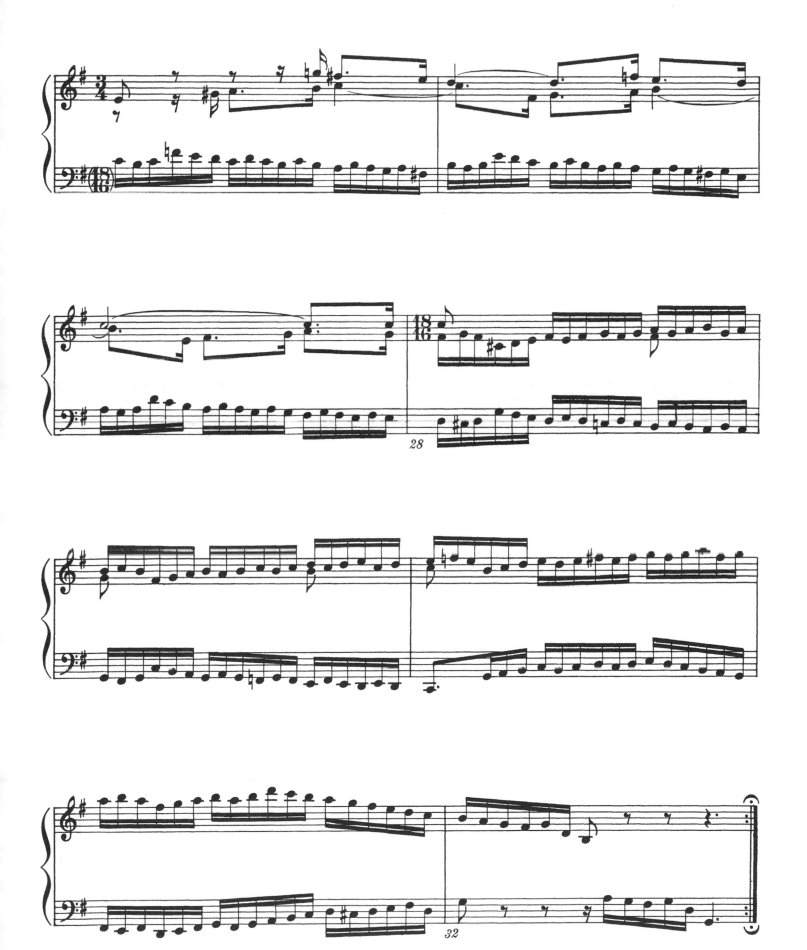

Variatio 27 Canone alla Nona a 2 Clav.

Variatio **28** a 2 Clav.

28

32

Variatio 29 a 1 ovvero 2 Clav.

Variatio 30 a 1 Clav. Quodlibet

Aria da Capo

Fine

TEXT REVISION

The text followed here is that of the original engraved edition published in Nürnberg by Balthasar Schmid. It might be remarked that this text is not as obscure as a few mistaken comments of Dannreuther[10] would imply, nor does it give reason to suspect the mistakes of which Forkel[11] complains: "Yet it must be remarked that in the engraved edition of these Variations are to be found several important mistakes, which the writer has carefully corrected in his copy."

The slightly inconsistent orthography of trills and mordents has been reduced to ∿ and ∿, the system of Couperin, thereby correcting the mistakes of the Bachgesellschaft edition, but in no way altering the original meaning. The dotted slurs and the ornaments in parenthesis were added to fulfill the obvious requirements of consistency. In Variation 5, Bar 22, C∿ has been suggested for ∿ of the original. In Variation 10, Bar 9, ∿ is suggested for ∿. In Variation 14, Bar 4, C∿ is read for the ambiguous sign in the original edition. In Variation 16, Bars 2, 3, 4, 5, 8, 11, the sign ⌐∿ should probably be interpreted as a *tremblement appuyé* and not as C∿, as in the Bachgesellschaft edition. However, the latter version is given in parentheses, since the original leaves room for hesitation. In Variation 20, Bars 15 and 31, the sign ∞ has been given in both places, because of the similar context. The engraving in the original is doubtless faulty, the turns being indicated somewhat ambiguously as § and ₰ , respectively. In Variation 21 the second sign in Bar 6 has been interpreted like those in Variation 16, and the preceding sign ∿ made to agree with it ∟∿.

In Variation 7, Bar 25, the Bachgesellschaft edition has B on the first beat of the right hand, instead of A as in the original.

In Variation 13, Bar 24, third beat, the E in the alto is misprinted as C in the original.

In Variation 16, Bar 21, the last E in the right hand is changed to F sharp in the Bachgesellschaft edition.

In Variation 23, Bar 27, the first and third upper notes in the right hand have been corrected as in the Bachgesellschaft edition to D from C of the original, obviously a misprint.

In Variation 25, Bar 13, in the original edition there is no sharp before the bass F in the last half of the second beat, as in the edition of the Bachgesellschaft.

In Variation 26, Bar 14, second beat, the original has misprinted D in the right hand instead of E.

The text has been transcribed into modern notation from the frequently changing clefs of the original. The realizations of ornaments and the one-keyboard versions of two-manual variations belong of course to this edition. So also do the dotted slurs and indications of voice leading, as well as all signs in parentheses. Occasionally rests have been added to clarify the voice structure where temporary silences of individual voices are not scrupulously indicated in full by the original. As there is no occasion here for divergence of opinion, parentheses have not been used.

Otherwise, if numerous proof-readings have accomplished their purpose, the text is true to the original.

---

[10]"Musical Ornamentation."

[11]"Über Johann Sebastian Bachs Leben, Kunst und Kunstwerke" IX.

EDITOR'S NOTE

In making an edition which shall faithfully reproduce the composer's original text and yet contain editorial explanations and indications for practical performance, one finds certain compromises inevitable. It has been the usual tradition either to try to impose a personal interpretation upon the text, or to make an even more vain attempt to compensate for inadequate musical education by the addition of numerous signs of phrasing, dynamics, *etc.*, in varying degrees of ingenuity, producing, in the rare instances when they are regarded by the amateur or student, only an empty travesty of musicianly performance, and gravely obscuring the text for the serious musician. It seems to me far better for the editor to treat with great discretion the author's text, for all its insufficiencies, than to add indications which bring with their own inadequacy the greater obscurity of doubtful authenticity.

How far the editor should go, and in what manner, depends somewhat on the character of the work. In view of the fact that even the clear, "unedited" Bach-gesellschaft version of the Goldberg Variations and its imitations contain mistakes in the ornamentation, a desire to establish at least one completely objective, accurate edition has led me to relegate to the preface, one after the other, the various categories of suggestions for performance. The symmetry of the Variations makes it easy in this case to suggest dynamics and tempo in the preface; the complete impossibility of indicating adequately on paper the subtleties of execution of a musical phrase made me abandon all recourse to signs of phrasing either conventional or invented, looking only to a general discussion of Bach phrasing in the preface, which, however inadequate to the subject, is at least no more futile than most editorial additions to texts. Only the idea of indicating fingering remained, finally to be abandoned when I realized the peculiarity of my own fingering and the doubtful value of a compromise which might well end by fitting the hand of no one. Especially in the canons the fingering originally de-

signed to guide the reading fingers of an amateur would be useless in its complexity, and in the performance of a musician most likely replaced by another. In spite of the enormous labor of creating and noting a consistent individual fingering, I felt that finally there is no cure for laziness but work! Therefore it seemed far better to leave the text free for each person to write in his own fingering.

However, for easier reference to realizations of the ornaments, and the execution of the two-keyboard variations on the pianoforte, alternate versions have been given above the original text where desirable. The arrangements of the two-keyboard variations are designed principally as a means to facilitate sight-reading. A glance at the original versions below will serve to make them musically intelligible. The serious performer observing simultaneously both versions, can easily work out his own fingering and division of notes between the hands to produce the clearest distinction between the voices.

Because of the general desuetude into which the original traditions of performance of ancient music have fallen, it seemed necessary to encroach upon the borders of a study work or a general discussion of the interpretation of Bach in describing, for example, the character of Bach's harpsichord and in expounding principles of ornamentation which in the eighteenth century were quite obvious. But it is hardly unfitting that attention to so many necessary but neglected details and principles should be provoked by Bach's supreme keyboard work.

For assistance in preparing this edition, warm thanks are due the following: Miss Eva J. O'Meara, of the Yale School of Music, for the facsimile of Bach's table of ornaments from the manuscript now there; Hans Dünnebeil, Berlin, for the loan of a copy of the first edition; Paul Boepple and Roger Sessions, for their valuable criticism of the preface; and all the others whose kindness and helpfulness both past and present has created a perpetual debt of gratitude.